STRING THEORY

FIRST EDITION, 2015

String Theory
© 2015 by Jenny Yang Cropp

ISBN 978-0-9903204-5-6

Except for fair use in reviews and/or scholarly considerations, no part of this book may be reproduced, performed, recorded, or otherwise transmitted without the written consent of the author and the permission of the publisher.

Cover Art
Multi-Variation 1
© 2015 by Michelle Johnson
http://www.mnartists.org/michelle-johnson

MONGREL EMPIRE PRESS
NORMAN, OK

ONLINE CATALOGUE: WWW.MONGRELEMPIRE.ORG

This publisher is a proud member of

[clmp]

COUNCIL OF LITERARY MAGAZINES & PRESSES
www.clmp.org

Book Design: Mongrel Empire Press using iWork Pages

STRING THEORY

Jenny Yang Cropp

2015

Acknowledgements

I would like to thank the editors of the following publications, in which these poems originally appeared:

Architrave Press: "At the Native American Film Festival"
Blue Earth Review: "Four and Twenty" and "Heavy Matter"
Boxcar Poetry Review: "Little Black Holes"
Eclipse: "Dragon in Snow" and "Orbit"
Ecotone: "Golgulsa"
Festival Writer: "Dark Energy, Dark Matter" and "When a Cloud Covers the Moon"
The Fiddleback: "The Visible Spectrum" and "Archer's Paradox"
Hayden's Ferry Review: "Oriental" and "Head of Dvarapalas"
Jelly Bucket: "Evangel," "Fellowship," and "Inpatient"
Literary Mama: "For My Mother, after Becoming a Mother"
The Oklahoma Review: "Stealing Kimchi"
Poetry City, USA: "Black Ice: Revisions"
Poetry Southeast: "String Theory"
Superstition Review: "Her Story," "Monsoon Season," and "On Those Nights I Didn't Die"

Special thanks to Jorge Evans and RockSaw Press, who published my chapbook, *Hanging the Moon*, in which some of these poems also appear. "Finding Samjokgo" appeared in a *P3: Poets, Painters, & Pavilion* exhibit and catalog at the Washington Pavilion of Arts and Science in Sioux Falls, South Dakota. "String Theory," "Native Speaker," "Little Black Holes," "Watching My Mother Make Kimchi," "Sijo for My Ten-year-old Self," "Sijo with Geese, Frost, and Moonlight," and "Hooker Hill" appear in *Nodin Poetry Anthology*, Nodin Press 2015. "Little Black Holes" was nominated for a Pushcart Prize.

Italicized lines in "Dark Energy, Dark Matter" come from *NASA* (http://science.nasa.gov/astrophysics/focus-areas/what-is-dark-energy/).

Acknowledgements

I'm grateful to all of the writers and mentors who inspired me and pushed me along the way, especially Honorée Fanonne Jeffers at the University of Oklahoma; Candace Black, Richard Robbins, and Richard Terrill at Minnesota State University-Mankato; and Lee Ann Roripaugh at the University of South Dakota. I owe a special thank you to Diana Joseph, Sarah Snook, and Danielle Starkey, writers and friends who kept me sane and kept me writing during my first years of motherhood, and to Jeanetta Calhoun Mish and Mongrel Empire Press for making this book possible.

CONTENTS

NATIVE SPEAKER	1
SIJO FOR MY TEN-YEAR-OLD SELF	2
AT THE NATIVE AMERICAN FILM FESTIVAL	3
WATCHING MY MOTHER MAKE KIMCHI	4
STEALING KIMCHI	5
ORIENTAL	6
DRAGON IN SNOW	7
MONSOON SEASON	8
HEAD OF DVARAPALAS	9
HOOKER HILL	10
GOLGULSA	11
LOWER MARKET	13
FINDING SAMJOKGO	14
FOOD FOR THE DEAD	15
HEAVY MATTER	22
HER STORY	23
EVANGEL	25
FELLOWSHIP	29
INPATIENT	30
APOLOGIA	31
ORBIT	32
TO MY FIRST GIRLFRIEND	33
WHEN A CLOUD COVERS THE MOON	34
TO MY RAPIST	36

FOUR AND TWENTY	37
ON THOSE NIGHTS I DIDN'T DIE	38
TO JOEL HENRY HINRICHS	39
BLACK ICE: REVISIONS	40
STRING THEORY	42
IN THE NURSERY	44
VISIBLE SPECTRUM	45
LITTLE BLACK HOLES	46
REFLECTION, REFRACTION, AND DISPERSION	47
DARK ENERGY, DARK MATTER	48
ARCHER'S PARADOX	49
SIJO WITH GEESE, FROST, AND MOONLIGHT	50
CAESAREAN	51
FOR MY MOTHER, AFTER BECOMING A MOTHER	52

for Phil and William

I.

The question is not how time speeds or slows for each of us,
relative to the rate at which we unravel our hearts.
The question is how we learn to vibrate at so many frequencies.

NATIVE SPEAKER

For fifteen years I've dreamed of halmoni's face.
And now, my grandmother is with me
in the back of this car. Uncle drives us through Seoul,
speeding and stopping, speeding again.
Palaces come and go. Aunt is on the phone,
trying to find someone who can translate
what they want from me. *You come back next year.*
You learn speak Korean. Halmoni taught me
how to say *hello, thank you,* and *grandmother*
when I was fourteen. I've forgotten all
but the last. She's gripping my hand and opening
a paper sack of grapes, bitter-skinned, full of seeds.
Frances. She says the only word she has for me,
my dead sister's name, then uses her one free hand
to feed us both. We need no one to translate
our silence or her slender fingers twining with mine,
how they won't let go, how they shift
under the weight of my palm.

SIJO FOR MY TEN-YEAR-OLD SELF

You don't know yet the names
      for all the faces you will carry,

carved out of wood, burned to ash
      and blown away. Remember this

when your teacher names you, calls you
      Chinese, makes you write haiku.

AT THE NATIVE AMERICAN FILM FESTIVAL

Marked at birth by a Mongolian blue spot,
mass of dark veins under thin skin, bruise-like
and only appearing on the backs of children
descended from Africa or Asia.
Next to my mother I am white, and
next to my father I am yellow.

But next to this Comanche woman
I am the spitting image of her daughter.
So when she asks about scholarships and schools,
when she wants to know if I'll attend
a college for native students, I think of the blue
born on her daughter's back. I let her look me
fully in my round face, let her think
I am part of something whole.

WATCHING MY MOTHER MAKE KIMCHI

Her body squat, bent in thirds, grips
the walls of a thick glass jar
holding in the red heat, its pale
veined leaves, fibrous cells beaten
to agility by rock salt and rinsed
clean to fit layer by layer. Between
each, a thick coat of crushed peppers
mixed into a paste. She won't tell me
the other ingredients, refuses
to let me come near enough, to see
the small cracks in her hands,
splits of skin in revolt. Instead, I hear
the grunt and sigh of her work. Trial
by raw flame. But we both know,
have known from birth, to stuff the jar
quietly, and not to flinch.

STEALING KIMCHI
For James

Fake flowers in vases, plastic and silk
scented red pepper, green onion,
garlic. Reminiscent
of my mother's kitchen, transient
except for the smell.
One summer with her
(if I was seven, my brother was five)
and then a void of senses after.
He and I sit quietly at this table
in a restaurant, remember
stealing kimchi from the fridge.
He, the crunchy parts,
and me, the soggy greens,
how the spice would linger in our hair.
Later, we learned the names, things
she did not have time to teach us:
dwaeji bulgogi with sticky rice,
doenjang and *baech'u* kimchi
wrapped in lettuce leaves.
Sukju namul, kimbap, mandu,
approximations of words, objects
we know more by sight and taste.
Food we eat with long pauses, slow
so the smell will follow us home.
Heat, sweat beading on our skin,
our child white hands lifting chopsticks.

ORIENTAL

The Wal-Mart cashier stares at my license, my face,
my license again, doesn't believe that's me
in the picture, eyes slanted because I smiled
too much, showed my teeth to the DMV. *You look
white in real life*, she says and inspects the photo
at different angles, intervals, degrees
of light. *Oriental*, she says, tapping one long
fake nail on her proof. She names me
the way we all must name the things we fear,
like she's picked me from a line-up, found me
hiding in plain sight. At first, I want to apologize,
offer an explanation, blame it on my mother
or my father, tell her about dominant and recessive
traits, my brother's coarse hair, my sister's eyes,
my round face. We can't help what we inherit—
the drunk at a party who thought it was safe
to pull his eyelids back and mock a Chinese taxi driver,
an ex who laughed when I wanted a bicycle
and asked if I'd be making deliveries, the Japanese
boss who frowned and shook her head
when I tried to commiserate. Our ability
to hold both sides in our skin makes no sense
to them, to this woman who repeats *oriental*
for emphasis after I've said I'm half-Korean,
as if I'm mistaken about which way the sun rises
or which direction I face, as if she's sure
when she takes my check, I'll go out to the parking lot,
untie my dragon, and fly away, due east.

DRAGON IN SNOW

Made from the language of precision, stitched
by tongue and lip, merging of vowel and
consonant, symbol and object, mother
and father swelling with love, love. Union,
birth, and naming. Now I move through the world
at 35,000 feet, fly south in winter, mark miles
by the shrinking snow. When the vast white
below me recedes to the shape of a dragon
billowing smoke, I remember the lines
of a dragon my father once colored for me.
I want to drop from the sky, body
dipped in red, fill the spaces between the lines
I've drawn. But somewhere ahead of me
there's a man who will brace my body
with his own, keep me from falling.
I will think I feel safe for the first time, forgive them
their sins. Measure twice and cut once
if you work with wood or stone, but flesh . . .
flesh cuts again and again.

MONSOON SEASON

When she asks me why I'm leaving,
I tell her about Korea, those five weeks

away, strange seduction in a *noribang*,
people singing, slurry of music, voices

sliding beneath closed doors,
and a man in black-framed glasses,

how I didn't know the word for *married*
and how the streets were bloated with rain.

I tell her about the taxi driver
who cheated me, how much I was willing

to pay, how I spent the rest of my trip
staring out my window, watching puddles

grow into mirrors for the shifting sun.
My last night, leaning over the sill,

I lit matches and dropped them,
counting the seconds it took

for each flame to fizzle out, not one
strong enough to light a path to the ground.

HEAD OF DVARAPALAS
Gyeongju National Museum, Republic of Korea

Give me a guardian with substance, face of stone
rage—cheekbones that jut, nose like cliff's edge,
stiff-spine eyebrows and pupils permanently dilated.
What enemies could he face in the dark
with fists that snatch dragons mid-air, top-knot
skimming clouds to catch lightning?

Give me more than a father's angels, gossamer
dissolved, orbs of light when I'm not looking.
I want mass and weight instead of bells and wings.

Give me my mother's history, Korea's sixth century
carved from rock, dreams worth protecting
with a guardian like this one, dug from mud
after a thousand years and still pissed off.

HOOKER HILL
Seoul, Republic of Korea

I go looking for the *m* attached to *other*,
missing letter still pressed against my forehead,
like she never said goodbye. I go there
to wander its alleys with eyes blearing under neon
and streetlight like a lost child stumbling
through grocery aisles, hungry and hoping
each hem I touch will be the one.

I go alone, dodging past the young girls
dressed like dolls, skimming men off sidewalks
and sucking them into the black and yawning
doorways. I head for even darker corners, climb up
into the past toward soot-layered buildings
and rusting pipes dating back before I was born,
to the older, solitary women standing idly
in dingy cuts of light, waiting for poorer,
hungrier men to find them.

I move through the dark, scanning their faces
until I find one who looks enough like me
that I feel less ashamed for staring.
She sits tilted in a straight-backed chair,
fanning her neck and her soft-spread thighs,
eyes fixed on the alley. I lean in to gaze
at the vaguely familiar, to find myself
etched in the web of stretch marks wrapped
around her exposed belly, but she brings
her hands forward to cover what she can,
to say there's nothing here for me,
that I should go now, stop looking.

GOLGULSA
Stone Buddha Temple, Republic of Korea

I'm not afraid of heights, but I am afraid of falling,
even more when Buddha's watching.

Where the stone steps narrow, slick and worn,
a rope hangs to pull yourself up
to the top of Mount Hamwol. There he sits,

waiting out the centuries, counting hands
and feet to mark the passing time.

I wonder if my mother climbed this mountain,
listened to the monks chanting breakfast,
showered in the morning rain, or felt this shame

like a tightness in the calves,
the pain of a climb to heights not meant for us.

Did she make her way to the top after praying
her goodbyes, then hear the devotion of bells
and feel hollow? Did she cling to the rocks,

unable to look up or down? I'll pretend
she took the same bus to get here, the 100 to Andong

crowded with students, arms aching
from holding a bar too high. She'd have worn
the wrong shoes, toes blistered

between the bus stop and the base of the mountain.
Near the top, lungs in flame, she'd have sat here,

in this alcove carved from stone, hidden
from Buddha's gaze. If I slip, he might laugh,
grateful for a break in the routine. Instead of a bow,

I could give him crushed bone. Instead of a chant,
he'd have my unconscious body.

This is all I've brought for an offering, the fruit
and flower of my fear, eternity of downward motion,

intimacy with gravity—mass acting on mass, forever,
without collision. I grip the rope knowing
we'll never compare notes, teeter on a wet rock ledge

and freeze where she froze, waiting to climb down,
for him to look the other way.

LOWER MARKET
Gyeongju, Republic of Korea

They mostly look away, the old women, or scowl openly,
but this one smiles up at me, crooked yellow teeth
between wrinkled lips stretched smooth. I smile back
and she rubs my arm. Beginning at the shoulder,
working down, she feels her way to my hand
and holds on for a moment as we stand side by side
at a crosswalk. This is her way of telling me
she approves of something she sees in my face.
I try to say thank you in Korean but the light changes
in my moment of forgetting, and she moves into the street.

FINDING SAMJOKGO

Unless you, too, have three legs and three claws, you will have to
concentrate, wrap yourself around each high, thin branch and frog-
kick your way through leaf and light, wince and wind

your fleshy palms around its splinters. Squeeze and scrape your thighs,
offering blood to the bark that will carry you up.
Unless you bring the gift of silence, go naked, go shivering.

Bring only the carving of your face for a mask, this pain and the next,
rings of feathers etched around your eyes. Forgive
your body for all the times it will have to fall

and ascend to learn that wood comes before fire, before ash. Forgive
not knowing which one you are, your wanting to be
jut and hollow, just a skin thickened by the sun.

On the uppermost branch of the uppermost tree, you will find
her or him, three shadows, and the one you
never wanted to see but dreamed of touching with fingers

shaped like wings. Call them to you with one word,
one name like an old song rising to greet you, returning
night's gift, a darkness wrapped in light.

FOOD FOR THE DEAD

"With a wooden spoon made from a willow tree, three spoonfuls of rice were fed to the corpse."
— *Korean Funeral Rites*

Dream in Which I Learn My Sister Is Dead

My grandfather wears a thin tie and small glasses, black-framed, his face a memory in grayscale, a photo I saw at his funeral, circa 1960s—preacher at the beginning instead of preacher at the end. Your subconscious knows more than you do, you the part and it the whole, gleaning answers to the *Times* crossword after they're published but before you've seen them. The body's slow release of information—zeros and ones streaming by, data without wisdom, filtered through flesh, lingering in muscle, trapped in fat, and only a few fired by synapse directly into the brain. He says he's come to reunite me with my family, and behind him a table is set: birthday cake, my name in pink buttercream, stacked plates, and a long line of Korean women waiting to feed me. A clear wall rises behind them, thick and soundproof, and a girl trapped on the other side pleads silently to come in. I won't read the headlines for ten more days, but while I sleep, news of her death goes out across the wire. One small photo all the papers will print passes through me. Sister at the end becomes girl behind glass, distorted, twisting into the familiar and out again, until I wake up, blood still ringing from the blare of her face.

Flushing teenager killed in two-girl knife fight

A man visiting his mother in Latimer Gardens hears shouting, gets up from their dinner, and from the window becomes a witness, an *according to* in my sister's story.

What happens to someone who watches a stranger die, left with unnamed grief, no funeral, no release?

He said she bled out in a boy's arms, but I know how much the papers don't print, the details left out, questions no one thought to ask. A boy died in front of my apartment once, and I had watched him all day pacing the sidewalk below my window, walked by him twice, passed him resting on the stairs, wanted to ask what he was waiting for. I waited too. Voices after midnight, shouts and shots and feet fleeing. My brothers sometimes shot soda cans off fence posts with pellet guns in the backyard. The only noise a distant clink, metal on metal, and the target fell to the grass. This boy fell, face-down on the sidewalk, arm tucked under his stomach. He bled out with a shotgun shoved in his back, an officer shouting, *Show me your hands.* A pager beeping underneath him.

Tell me what the story doesn't say: last words she heard or said, how a blade dulled by bone sounds striking asphalt, the circumference of her blood, if the man in the window went back to his dinner and finished eating, how much space the silence must have filled after the sirens were turned off.

Hills Without Jars

It's 3 am in Tennessee. My brother's been driving all night because he doesn't like how I swerve slightly to the left when I check my blind spot, how my hands follow where my head goes. He plans to take us all the way to New York and our sister's grave on cigarettes and antacids. Later, he'll dry-heave in a truck stop men's room. I'll punch the button on a dryer mounted to the thin wall between us, turn its nozzle up so the hot air fills my ears. I'll buy crackers, leave them open but uneaten, tell him I've lost my appetite counting road kill, too many red splotches passing by like highway signs: Morbidity - Next 4 Exits, Awkward Silence - 35 miles.

He'll ask me what I think about death, and I'll remember the night after our grandfather died. We sat in his car in the driveway, waiting for the saddest part of a song to make us cry. All I know about death is grief, but he's sure there's nothing after, that ghosts only haunt the eyes that need to see.

Near dawn, he'll grow tired and let me drive. I'll watch the hills rolling us toward the Atlantic and the faces of our dead, my own in the windshield fading in the rising light.

Three Spoonfuls

When I can't look at her grave anymore, I look at the people buried next to my sister, two brothers killed in The World War. Imagine thinking something like that would never happen again.

After their funerals, women would have rolled up their sleeves and stood shoulder to shoulder in a small kitchen chopping onions, peeling potatoes, each with her own story about a parent who lost a child that year, each keeping her hands busy with the business of grief. I light one cigarette with the butt of another, squash and stuff it in my pocket. We're two weeks late, and there's nothing to do but stare at the mound of flowers wilting into each other. I'd like to sleep through the middle of this moment or start over, not stop for burgers on the way, reshape the memory so the graveyard won't smell like meat and grease.

I'd like to be alone here instead of watching my brother take pictures he'll send later with no note, instead of watching my mother tuck cookies between the roses and ribbons, offering food for the dead like she was taught—strawberry, shortbread, and silence—the same sweet end she'll offer us on the way home.

II.

And again and again this ache inside you will seem to come
sudden and strange, but how hard you are willing to love, how long
you can hold on, is written in the universe of your body.

HEAVY MATTER

This is the time for talking to God. This body,
light and eager to bend at the knee,
once gave up weight in prayer.

And this mind, before its loss of faith,
believed its burden was lifted.
Now I feel a pressing down, life's gravity.

My father says empty beds are good
for disappearing. He can stretch out,
spread his arms and legs, lose the tips

of toes and fingers, then hands and feet.
Like da Vinci's sketch of man, a range
of human lines, blurred edges. But the body

is made up of heavy matter, remnants
of a supernova—iron, carbon, calcium—
slung together. When I can't sleep

I fear death and want to pray,
brace myself, shift weight from hip to hip,
rock my body to a tune. *Do, Lord.*

Oh, do, Lord. Like my grandmother singing
hymns in her rocker, crocheting blankets
and then unraveling the stitches.

The day her husband died, she baked a pie—
lemon meringue, egg whites beaten to stiff peaks
by hand. That night, she cut one slice

and threw the rest away. When I can't sleep,
I suffer that slow drift, the spreading
of the universe, the breaking down of things.

HER STORY

Her grandmother thinks she talks too much, this twelve-year-old
who sits with me after church at the kid's table because I'm like her,
not from here, just visiting, and she draws a map to show me

where she's from, her baby fat fingers turning pink at the creases,
pen tip tearing through layers of napkin. That's her house

by the ketchup stain, and two doors down, an aunt and uncle,
a few cousins there and more in a trailer nearby, but they play
with her brothers mostly. She works in her dad's store selling bait

after school, doesn't mind touching worms or minnows,
will even bait her own hook. She points a French fry at the store,

less than a mile from home, says two girl cousins her own age
live right behind it, and sometimes they go fishing at the lake,
or they used to but they can't anymore, not alone and not just girls.

I remember what it's like to be a child, a girl child, seen
but not heard, so I smile when she asks if I like fishing and if

I've been to that lake, seen the fog that rises up off the surface
at sunset after a long, hot day, but she's not looking at me.
She's watching her grandmother who thinks a smart girl ought to know

when to leave well enough alone, but the woman's got a mouthful
of someone's potluck casserole and can't hear when she chews,

so the girl shoves the sleeves of her big red sweatshirt up, the one
she changed into as soon as the service was over, and leans in
to tell me the thing she's not supposed to talk about.

Last summer, she says, she went to the lake every morning by herself,
to get away from her brothers, and that's how she found the truck,

because it was there one day, which didn't mean anything,
but it was still there the next morning and the next, and the door
on the driver's side was always open, no one in there, and the tires sank

a little each day into the sand, and it was two boys, sure,
cousins on her dad's side, who found the body later, in the trees,

but they're still allowed to go out there, to the place she's forbidden
and marks for me on the map, three lines and a leaf next to a swirl
of blue ink and a sprinkle of salt near the water's edge

where her own brothers found the knife, at least that's how they tell it,
even though it was her, she was the one who saw the blood.

EVANGEL

1. Communion

Once a month and on holidays, heavy sheen
of silver, polished cross on a domed lid, doll-sized
cups, each fitting its own secure circle, passed
from mouth to mouth. She filled the cups
on Saturday night with Welch's grape juice, broke
sheets of Keebler crackers into tiny slivers
and thought about the pews, heavy
and hand-crafted, crosses carved into the sides,
preacher's tolling, keeping time with his fist,
hallelujah and *thank-you-Jesus,* varnished oak
sticking to her legs, how her knees bruise
when she prays. She poured the juice and portioned
crackers as her salted lips and tongue imagined
how the body would taste in the morning,
how the blood was barely enough to wash it down.

2. Celestial

Because nothing else worked as well, not God
who wanted everything, or the father who wanted nothing,
or tying red yarn around her finger to remember
the clothes left drying, hung on the line. Because she twisted
and tightened, worried her skin to deeper and deeper shades,
but the rain came anyway, even when the air was dry, even
when she prayed and slept and starved. Because she was left
so often wet and hungry, she wondered if it was possible
to spin like a star circling hot and fast, to make something
of her own heat, to burn her garments dry.

3. Penance

She waited years for a sign, the usual lightning bolt
or burning bush that never came, a blinding light
or trumpets. She waited for angels with fiery swords,
blizzard of feathers. Her skin still cracks and blisters
when glass plays catch with the sun, stray beams
tossed back and forth until one gets loose,
touches her face. *What's done is done*, the preacher said.
And some things can't be undone. Her father's body
in the kitchen, screen door slamming in the wind,
no one to latch it shut. She prayed to take it back,
but her bruised knees never healed, and still
she can smell the blood that seeped from her feet
as she stood in the sun for hours, barefoot, burning.

4. Revival

She went looking for her father's hands, hands that built things,
broke things, cupped her mother's hips. One hand landed
on her cheek like the hard pillow of a grade school desk.
Mrs. Otipoby, round as her name, had turned out the lights,
told them to imagine their favorite places. Inside, in the dark,
in the dust of her father's study, she weighed the heft of his pen
on her palm, eyes closed, like it might hold what's still
unwritten about love, like it might know something
about locked drawers, let her pry them open now he's gone
and sort through all the unmarked keys.

FELLOWSHIP

Old men want coffee and boys want
the waitress who smells like liquor, like suede
on a hot day, though they don't know why.

The waitress wants a break, and the mothers are watching.

Two cats mate in the weeds at the farthest edge
of the parking lot, sun-bleached streets cornering,
framing, and the girls stare at their shoes—gloss dimmed,
scuffed—or stare out the window, planning
for later, when they'll need some shade.

Which thin shadows under which thin eaves?

They look and look away. They sit back to back,
a stay against temptation, hands locked
neatly in laps or held down beneath thighs

to keep fingers in want of use from reaching

toward the nearest body not their own. They daydream
a new scripture, new words they can take to bed and wake
feeling like they learned something that can't be unlearned,
like they touched heaven's hem and knew
how the seams were sewn, felt each stitch

closing them up, making them whole and heavy, able

to hold it all in like wood doors swinging into place
under their own weight, like a web of roots
under the long grass, under the big sky,

pinning down the dirt, sealing shut their open graves.

INPATIENT

An old man sings Sinatra to keep me there,
in a courtyard of fence and concrete,
plastic table and chairs, pebbles where flowers
might have grown, so I light up again, singe clean,
new paper with the last heat of ash, watch him
find my face behind smoke. Between each note,
a promise. *When we get out of here*, he says,
I'm going to marry you. That first night he kicked
every nurse who got near him, but now he's quiet,
now he sleeps. Now he spends his days
writing me love letters in crayon, remembering
words he thought he lost.
       In therapy,
we go round and round. Today we're me,
we're reliving my life. My mother has us trapped
in a bedroom. No bed. Toys and clothes piled
here and there like small burial mounds. We play
tic-tac-toe on the carpet, fingers dragging circles
into the stiff fibers. Everyone here has a mother—
living, missing, dead—messing with our lives.
Today, our mother is running. Our stepfather is
chasing her into the bedroom, his breath
blunt as fists. She's swift to pick us up, shield
her own face, her jagged nails digging in the soft
skin of our arms. With one pair of eyes,
we wince.
  When it's over, I wait outside
for another song. There's a ring in Sicily,
the old man says. Four carats, pear-shaped and pink,
some land, lots of land, and his favorite aunt
who could make four courses out of bread and wine.
When we get out of here, he tells me, *we'll feast.*

APOLOGIA

Fall's beauty doesn't move me. I find
the way one color recedes, exposing
another (green chlorophyll

giving way to red anthocyanin,
red to yellow xanthophyl, orange
carotene, and finally, all of it ending

in the brown of empty cells, waste
breaking down) too scientific,
not enough wonder.

I worship at the altar of unknown things,
practice the karma of hearts
and cigarettes, always giving when asked,

even if it's my last one.

ORBIT

His wife says he loves you. He thinks
you hung the moon. Seventeen and all you know
is that stars take longer, and what then? You're gone,
off to college when she's off her meds, trying
to time the light so no one sees.
Something always drops from the sky
when you're not looking, and a small mass
hurtles toward Earth, falling down and down
until it meets resistance. After finals and his divorce,
you learn the truth is, she was jealous of you,
or so he says, his hands planted
on your shoulders. You should have
told his wife about the falling, about the leaves
and rain and stones, how mountains let go,
clouds let go, even axils between stems
and branches weaken and release. We fall
by force, attraction, gravity. That's how we meet
in pools of water and piles of leaves. That's how
we love in damp stretches of grass and debris.
You could have told her about the moon,
how it was never meant for him, but something
dropped, and you were new to collision.
What did you know about hanging the moon,
how it escapes its falling, how it moves
away at constant speed?

TO MY FIRST GIRLFRIEND

I have now known women more broken than you.
They send their love and want to know
if those Pakistani boys still whisper sweet, their skin
begging to touch you where I touched you,
in daylight, with their hands. But they were
tongues in the night, quick and disembodied, means
to an end. I think I get it now. I was privileged
finger in your mouth, cradler of hips. Like Pyrex,
so often dropped and barely chipped, you
could hold such heat in your black leather
jacket, heavy silver rings on every finger
for protection, for each man in your past you needed
to hate. It hurt too much to hold your hand.

WHEN A CLOUD COVERS THE MOON

The field goes blank. I can't tell
my limbs from the sky. I can't tell

your voice from a rusty creak,
a gate swinging open and shut, or is it

the low roll of a tractor
weighed down by a round bale of hay?

You can't hear me. My words get lost
in a whistle of fear and wind.

In the dark, I am erased,
except for my fingers, still hot

from the bale, fresh cut hay
compressed, each piece bound tight

to another, friction and moisture
building heat. This is how

barn fires start—a smoldering
deep inside the bale, unnoticed

until it's full flame. This is why
later, trying to ease ourselves to sleep

in a camper near the woods,
far from house and porch light,

swarms of mosquitoes
shadowing the front garden,

we'll lose each other again, edges
blurring and fading. In the dark,
breath and heat. Our turn and press
singeing mattress and blankets,

windows of thick plastic
melting under our touch.

TO MY RAPIST

We skinny-dipped the Canadian River,
six-packs in foam coolers on the bank, footprints
in red mud headed upstream through the dark,
water lapping where we edged ourselves
into the current. We floated on our backs,
watched the moon climb high enough
to expose bare limbs breaking the river's surface.
Why not homicidal thoughts? My therapist suggested
I redirect anger outward. It would make more sense.
But faith is a naked girl wrapped in a blanket,
and shame goes down like shots of hard liquor
when the beer runs out. It hits you
all at once, and I did say yes to that last one,
yes when you wanted to stay, yes to hold me, yes
to sleep. Now I dream the river killed you,
carried you to Eufala Lake, slammed your head
against the dam. I dream wet bodies and warm fire,
waving goodbye when you ask if you can float
all the way to Arkansas, moonlight catching the round
of a whiskey bottle in your hand, yes, yes.

FOUR AND TWENTY

Grief takes me like this, when it wants,
now, parked outside an Arby's.
I press my face against the car window,

count the birds, two dozen, small and blue-black,
perched wing to wing on the red glow
of a neon tube, their own street corner

high above the snow. I want them to sing me back
to nursery rhymes, days of rye, but these tough,
hard birds still hold trophies of human flesh

tucked beneath each wing, so I wait
to see if one will fly and let go the maid,
to see her dissolve midair.

ON THOSE NIGHTS I DIDN'T DIE

I was close enough to death to remember laughter
echoing through my body, hollow, pushing
skin until it stretched to bursting,
though perhaps those few seconds when I thought
I was done, it was all in my head.
Sometimes it was more like a dream, and I was vapor
expanding in panic, drifting out and out
until I woke up heavy and solid,
and you'd think death would be harder to remove,
but consciousness, each time I tried to lose it,
returned like a spasm of regret, like a sudden intake
of breath, electric shock of relief, even with
an eternity of starlight pressing shut my eyes,
even as I stared into the vein-red distance.

TO JOEL HENRY HINRICHS

You didn't know me. You were a friend of a friend
who never knew my name, whose name I never heard
until you exploded, a fine mist of blood and chemical

and ash against the microbiology building
where I failed botany five times, on the bench
where I wept and plotted my own demise—

not nearly as spectacular as your backpack bomb.
It shook the stadium that night, and 84,000 football fans
felt it, paused for a moment, and then went on cheering,

their voices unable to match your sonic boom, fading
after a few blocks while yours carried five miles.
The bench was gone by morning, smooth

worn gray replaced with fresh, raw wood, your flesh
on the sidewalk power-washed away.
In the flowerbeds, pieces too small to collect, blood

too quickly soaked up by dirt. In the spring, I sat
on the bench, felt the splinters bite my thighs,
enjoyed the flowers blooming, owing you their lives.

BLACK ICE: REVISIONS

I am watching my grandfather die. I am watching my father who is watching his father die. I am telling you this as if it were true, but it's not. If I say it again, then maybe, but more likely this is a poem where I try to convince myself that I am there, watching as the liver shuts down, as he drifts and kicks, flings sheets from skin, moans *glory to God* to hear it echo in what space he has left, to pass a message father to son, father to son. But I am not a son, and I am not there. I am a week before this, high on a concrete floor, dipping my toes in a pile of ash. Or am I a week before that, too wasted to come out of the dark? And if I say it again? I am watching my grandfather die. I am watching my father and can't help thinking about how he'll die, maybe the same way, slow creep of toxins through the body, his own child watching and waiting, resting in a bedside chair. But I am still not there. I do not see my face reflected in a bedroom window, because there was never a bedroom window, because this poem is a made thing and he is not dying at home. He is already dead, and I am still not there. I am not watching my father or my grandfather or my face in the blear of a public bathroom mirror. I am not reading the front page of the paper on the morning he finally died, its caption about an ice storm that barely missed us. I am not resting my solace on a metaphor about black ice, slick and deceiving. This is not memory or time travel. If he's already gone, then where am I? If I'm no good with my grief, then where am I? I am saying no to a boy who wants to love me. I am saying no because his love is a just a fear of dying, and I am busy not being there. I am counting my own pills. I am repeating to myself, *After this, after this, I quit.*

III.

Orion, I'll say, when it's time to point up, to show you how
stars that seem to cluster are hundreds of years apart, how time
is distance, and they, like you, are growing away from me.

STRING THEORY

Pluck the rubber band of existence
and suddenly my dead sister is risen,
sharpening knives in the kitchen

and waiting for me to find her,
because it is possible
that there are no new particles,

only the same ones we've already seen.

Imagine a string instead of a particle,
and then think,
think about frequency,

how the same string can make so many sounds.

Then my mother's missing breast
hums back into existence as my own,

the single stalk of bamboo I killed last year
springs to life
in a molecule of water,

and the sheets from all my childhood beds combine
to hold me in quiet sleep.
Pluck the string again, and the vibrations

could erase our most private moments of pain
or re-create the place where they happened, this time
in daylight, the edges filled with witnesses.

And if I find just the right chord,
those cruel fingers that tore me open
might vibrate into a million grains of pollen

and be carried off for something useful

while the universe
is again a moving, breathing thing, a fluctuation
in and out of possibility.

IN THE NURSERY

We sometimes say exactly what we mean,

and in her utterance, I was flesh undone,
made into a wish, dust and gas
in the vacuum of space,

waiting my turn to become

the body's language, forward momentum
of heartbeat and bone.
I was, in that moment, an impossible

stillness, a dream at absolute rest.

VISIBLE SPECTRUM

I am two halves of the moon, the waxing and the waning,
never whole, never new, reflection of twin suns, one coming
and one going, and where the road bends, heads east
to face the morning, dark veil slipping further and further
back, the light cuts. No quid pro quo. No offer
in my upturned hand. You are what I am, woman who forgot
her own childhood, who stands in the yard
with her camera, documents rainbows dancing at the edge
of her sprinklers, dilating. We are the light
and the prism, the beautiful and the suspect. I am the child
who knows, and you are the knowing,
why she runs from light switch to bed but keeps her eyes
open, waits for the wall of dark to dissolve.
We are the moon that disappoints and street lights
blinking their hazy yellow, their long-short-long, some
dotting corners, others outlining whole cities,
and between the lines, headlights in motion, coming of white,
going of red, and at every start and every finish
a window glowing, a bedside lamp, a flashlight
beneath the blanket, blinking neon signs
and naked bulbs swinging from their wires, all
leaking our dim light into pools visible from space. We are
the child who calls them to her, who knows how far we came
and sees the dark distance still untraveled.

LITTLE BLACK HOLES

"... could be drifting around our solar system like dust motes in an old house." –*San Francisco Chronicle*, July 2006

Finally, something to blame for lonely socks
and missing lighters. They lurk in closets
eating spiders and old photos at will

while others sneak out at night, run tabs
at the bar, then sneak back
into my brain to dine on dendritic spines,

so it's not my fault I can't remember
my mother's birthday or the names
of all the boys and girls I've kissed.

When my boyfriend asks for the book
I borrowed and lost, I will tell him
subatomic black holes exist, and they take

what they want—memories, dreams,
minutes of precious sleep. We'll have to hide
the things we want to keep, not the whiskey night,

but the night before that, its splintered porch,
beans simmering slowly upstairs, one light
in the alley stacking wood, shadow, wood.

We can leave the rest sitting out—drunk fights,
ex-wives, whatever settles in the space
between our fears. Stack them neatly

in the corner or at the foot of our bed,
wait for the holes to feast,
watch our offerings disappear.

REFLECTION, REFRACTION, AND DISPERSION

Where the curb slopes to meet the crosswalk,
someone has tossed away a carton of milk,
half-full, its contents spilling,
joining the rain. Iridescent,
this delicate blue-white vein, light
within substance, pours itself into the street.

DARK ENERGY, DARK MATTER

1. No one expected this, no one knew how to explain it. But something was causing it.

From the empty lot across the street, I sketch my house, an empty frame with darkened windows. Charcoal smudges and becomes shadow. My fingers for erasers. It isn't life or time, fate or family, which rubs until my edges blur and fill the page. Destroy and create. Destroy and create.

2. Maybe there was some strange kind of energy-fluid that filled space.

I want my son to learn to swim. Summers, I floated on my back in bodies of water green and dark or bobbed in the shadows of wooden docks. Horse flies and splinters. Hours spent heaving myself up into the sun, then jumping back in. In the movement from water to air, the body learns how heavy it is.

3. More is unknown than is known.

Always a hum instead of silence. Cricket or wind, electric feedback, whistle and echo, pulse or breath. But, to be still? To feel the universe expand but not have to hear it?

4. The number came out 10^{120} times too big. That's a 1 with 120 zeros after it. It's hard to get an answer that bad.

Even a physicist must sometimes mistake pain for love, wonder later at how easy it is to be so wrong.

ARCHER'S PARADOX
For Diana

It's not enough to aim
and release, to follow procedure,

placement of arrow, placement of fingers, pulling
back on a tight tight string. Is it called a string?

I never know what I'm aiming at
until it's bleeding its last breath.

Today, a southern gust shoves me
onto the shoulder so I'm forced to drive

for miles, wheels turned left
to correct, curving to follow a straight line.

Stiffer spines fly better
from a stronger bow.

These arrows are flimsy things,
my string a string of daydreams. I need

you and me on a couch on a porch, blowing
smoke at the winds. They push us

that way and this, two girls
never taught how to hunt, fascinated

by failed marriages, the means and ways
our bodies have been bowed.

But you say it's okay to miss,
to make a mess sometimes.

You say when we're ready for dead
center, we'll know how to aim to the side.

SIJO WITH GEESE, FROST, AND MOONLIGHT

By geese, I meant a pink couch
      turned gray, then gold, as the sun set.

By moonlight, I meant my face,
      turned away. The frost was a lie,

an open window, a body
      waiting, an empty field, me.

CAESAREAN

Bee sting needle. Electric ping and spine
song and numb. No more splitting of bone,
guttural moan and wrench.

But numb is something too. Not lack of
sensation but severed relationships,
nerves draped with grief,

telling stories, nostalgic. I can't feel my feet,
but they still remember,
fifteen years ago, tapping soft tunes

at the edge of a pebbled river, silt between the toes,
a whole night spent in awe
of the moon, ankles ever slender

entering the water over and over.
Above the belly, now,
the body shivers, bends to its own defeat,

to the morphine and the cold, metallic
absence of smell, to the papered people
shuffling mumbles back and forth, one disembodied

voice and then another and then my own, breasts
hung like Roman scales weighing
an ounce of milk against a pound of gold,

palms up, supplicating, open to a sudden love
of tyranny, arms ecstatic to be
strapped down when they make the emperor's cut.

FOR MY MOTHER, AFTER BECOMING A MOTHER

Because it's two o'clock in the morning and my son's been up for hours and my arms are heavy tired and he can't look at me yet, can't smile, can't coo, can't do much but eat and crap and complain, I think, *You don't look anything like me. You can't be mine. You don't belong to me.*

How hard it must have been for her, nineteen, alone for weeks at a time while her husband soldiered in the field.

Tiny apartment.
Two babies crying.
Two mouths gaping wide with their own primal grief, four lips set against her.

She paced and chain-smoked, swallowed uppers, watched the clock, and when we slept, or when she thought we slept, or when she stopped caring if we slept, she cracked open can after can after can.

Even now, I salivate when someone opens a beer.

It takes both hands to breastfeed. To dial the phone, I have to choose between letting go of my breast or letting go of my baby.

Me: *There's a baby hanging from my breast. I had to tell someone.*
Someone: *It's okay. You're okay.*
Me: *What is it about being a mother that makes me long for mine?*
Someone: *It's okay. You're okay.*

No one knows how long she was gone before my father came home from field exercises. He'd been gone for days. She took half their stuff but left the babies.

Both eyes closed, I dial from memory.

Me: *Did you get the photos? Did you see your grandson?*
Her: *Yes, but I don't know what to say. That's why I don't call.*
Me: *I just wanted to make sure you got the photos. You saw them?*
Her: *Yes, but I don't know what to say. That's why.*
Me: *Okay.*
Her: *He looks like his father.*

The year I drop out of college, I rent an apartment in the same complex where my parents lived just after I was born. It has an avocado-green fridge. It's across the street from Gibson's Discount Center. Most days, while my father was at work, my mother went there to walk the aisles and imagine all the things she'd buy if (*when*) she had more money. She left me at home.

When I lose my job, I go there, too, to see all the things she never bought: gold-plated barrettes, headbands with thick plastic teeth, Love's Baby Soft, denim skirts with studded hems, patent leather heels, gauzy summer blouses with eyelet lace on the sleeves, peach shampoo, sweet almond lotion, thirty shades of Revlon nail polish and their matching lipsticks, hard-sided suitcases she would need to pack these things and take them with her.

It takes months to touch each object.

Her brother took the photo when he went to visit her at the orphanage. My mother as a young girl in Korea, her family too poor to keep her. Their mother must have been off to the side or behind him as he framed the shot, as he told his little sister to duck down so he could watch her emerge from the weeds. I wonder if he told her to smile, told her to pretend she was running toward them. How many weeks or months later did she run away?

It sat on an end table, next to a black leather couch in an anonymous high-rise in Queens, a one-bedroom she shared with her mother (bamboo mat rolled and stowed in a corner) and her two other daughters (some weekends, blankets on the floor) and then my brother and I (just this once, tucked between our sisters at night).

Downstairs, in the lobby, another couch, a boy I met at an arcade who slipped his hand beneath the damp edge of my swimsuit and said, "I'm nineteen. How old are you?"

The same age my mother was in that photograph with her Catholic school-girl uniform, her thin smile—hard lines in a field of tall grass.

Too young.

We are lying on the floor, and my son is staring up and out at the world, not at me, but at something just beyond me, and for a moment he's calm, mesmerized, almost happy. Then the moment is gone. He scrunches up his face and wails, and I think, *When you're sad, your face looks just like mine.*

When he's sad, I know he belongs to me, to our mutual frustration. It's as if he knows how hard I'm trying to change the circumstances of our births.

Whenever he cries like this, I want to cry too, but instead, I pick him up and pat his back. "It's okay," I say. "You're okay." Over and over until he falls asleep.

Author Photo by Melissa Hall—Lighthouse Studio

Jenny Yang Cropp grew up mainly in Oklahoma. She attended the University of Oklahoma, where she received her B.A., and Minnesota State University-Mankato, where she received her M.F.A. in creative writing. She is currently completing a Ph.D. in English at the University of South Dakota. She lives in Lawton, Oklahoma, with her husband and son, and she teaches English at Cameron University.

www.ingramcontent.com/pod-product-compliance
Lightning Source LLC
LaVergne TN
LVHW041309080426
835510LV00009B/915